Saint Peter and the Goldfinch

Saint Peter

and

the

Goldfinch

Poems by
Jack Ridl

WAYNE STATE UNIVERSITY PRESS
Detroit

MADE IN MICHIGAN WRITERS SERIES

GENERAL EDITORS

Michael Delp, Interlochen Center for the Arts
M. L. Liebler, Wayne State University

A complete listing of the books in this series can be found online at
wsupress.wayne.edu

ISBN 978-0-8143-4645-7 (paperback)
ISBN 978-0-8143-4646-4 (e-book)

Library of Congress Control Number: 2018959986

Publication of this book was made possible by a generous gift from The
Meijer Foundation. This work is supported in part by an award from the
Michigan Council for Arts and Cultural Affairs.

Wayne State University Press
Leonard N. Simons Building
4809 Woodward Avenue
Detroit, Michigan 48201–1309

Visit us online at wsupress.wayne.edu

For Julie, Meridith, and Betsy

Contents

The Man Who Decided to See

The Long Married

Waiting for the Astronomer

The Train Home

It Was Last Night, I Think

During the storm,
I wondered
about gathering
all the drops.
From there it
took off into all
this other stuff: light
on the underside
of leaves, what
rust peels away,
the space between
musical notes. I forgot
what time it was; I
wrote that down.
When I was a kid
I loved plus signs
and hummingbirds
in the honeysuckle.
I have jars filled
with words my
father left behind.

Wondering What It Was Like

Walking around our little town, I would
look at the front doors, sometimes see
a figure walking past a window, sometimes

watch as a light was turned out. Once, invited
to a friend's farm after school, riding the bus
to his stop and then walking across the snow

to his front porch and then walking in and
seeing his mother reading a book, I felt
something in my blood. She hugged us,

told us to hang up our coats, and
come have a "little something to tide you
over until dinner." Something in that house

calmed every word. Something lay calm
on everything: the broom leaning against
the sink, the pot on the stove, the tables,

cups, books; peace even seemed to lie within
the rugs. His mother called us to the window
and said, "Look!" There was a male cardinal,

black chin against its violent red, sitting
on a snow-covered branch. And then I saw
the tractor, snow piled on its metal seat,

and then the wind-sculpted snow drifts.

American Suite for a Lost Daughter

I am the last greylag on the left side of the V.

I am the amen in the prayer you never say.

I can bring some stones to you, to the place
you left as a child, the place where the wolves
came to drink and watch you. They watched
you through eyes set deep in the land.

Here you wait, while the dark moon
keeps to its path and the owl watches
the rabbit sit beneath the net of hollow stars.

Christ did not read palms; his lonely
eyes saw the way the lightning grazed
the sky and shot the mind full of questions.
His heart was the color of the center of a tangerine.
His hands lived alone.

Somewhere in any city is a late-night
disc jockey looking out the window
to his left, thinking about the bills
he pays, the children he cannot raise,
the wife he tries to love because he wants
to love her, and this madness we call
music as it moves out and into the dark air.

You came through a tunnel that began
in the mind's assent to the ancient gnaw.
Your walk has grown from the terrible
chance. Your voice rises and adds its
being to the winds, to that of the piano
and machine gun, the cruel demand and
the long withdrawing sigh of your strange question.

I try to dream your dreams—to let
my mind enter yours and live the intrusions
that keep you from everything you should have.
I find the song we all sing.

I am thinking again of distances.

Your brother came alone
amid the streaks of sun.
He tosses balls; he somersaults.
You were once so little you
could become an arch; bent
backwards, you could walk
around our yard. You could
sit, spread your legs, lean
your forehead into the cool summer grass.

Brahms on the stereo.
You on your bicycle.

I knew your great-uncle Mac.
He would always hold the chair
for Aunt Fan. He loved raking leaves.
Some days I think of all the dead
you can never know. Some days they
are a cloud moving over your own roof.

When you were seven, I suddenly
became "Dad." I wondered
if I should tell you then how far
I was from being a father.

In our herb garden grow thyme,
marjoram, rosemary, lemon balm,
and a weed we named white whisper.

The night, like an idiot savant, does
over and over its one miraculous task.

I want us to be important
for no reason at all.

Then I think of you, broken
and stunned, sitting alone, your
life taken and the only thing left
whatever clings to your mind,
you near death, wondering still
why this terrible life had to be
lived within.

I would pray for your life if I could.

Yesterday, as two planes collided
and fell across several Southern
California homes, bodies flung
through the cool breeze and slammed
into the ground, I thought of the wound
between us, how it will never heal, how
impossible it has become to sense
or gauge the pain that hurls itself
across this age of circumstances no one
can recover from. Prayer. Prayer.

If none of this can bring a god to
end it all, then . . . I remember
the nights we walked and tried
to see only the stars.

While the Dog Sleeps

It's the birthday of Stephen Crane.
On this date, Michelangelo said yes
to the pope and gathered his brushes.

At the church next door, the choir
is rehearsing. There is nothing
I want to rehearse. Recently I've

been realizing, "If that didn't exist, I
would never miss it." I say it a lot.
But not about you. We put isinglass

over the screens on the porch so we
could sit there in sweaters, take the time
to see what was in front of us. Now

"tomorrow" is a strange word, "now"
even stranger. "Yesterday" makes sense,
but not much of it is true. Our dog still

keeps sleep. I imagine him dreaming
la dolce far niente. When asked
if I miss what I did for forty years

I like to say, "That never existed."
Now here on the porch I take in the light
crossing the last leaves doing their slow

dance in the breeze, watch the chickadees
at the feeder, once in a while glance at
the sundial we set in the shade of the redbud.

Garage Sale

She asked me to carry his clothes
from their closet to the clothesline

she had, for her garage sale, strung
from the backyard fence to a hook

on the side of their house. He was
a friend. In their bedroom his clothes

hung on the top pole, hers on the pole
beneath: everything draped from wire

hangers, the kind that come back
from the dry cleaners. I lifted off

a dozen shirts, half a dozen pairs of
corduroy pants and headed down

the stairs. I couldn't see each step.
She held the back door open and

when I hung the clothes, the line drooped,

the center sagging to the driveway. She
said, "You have to balance them."

Is It Virginia Woolf I'm Thinking Of?

The wisteria branches hang twisted through, over,
and out from the pergola and it's Christmas. They
will bend and stay until May. Then we will prune
them into some semblance of place. In the kitchen

there are cheeses on the Santa plate, the one where
he is walking toward his sleigh, sack hung full
over his back. I wonder about taking a slice
of gouda. I can't remember if we are going out

to someone's for dinner or if someone is coming
here for wine and cheese, crackers and talk. It's
midafternoon. Maybe it's the neighbors coming
here. I think we invited them. I'll play it safe.

Instead, I'll water the tree. The cat likes to drink
from the stand. The tree is nine feet tall, the tallest
tree we have ever had, and I balanced myself
on the third step of the three-step step stool and

placed the star. Outside, the predicted ice storm
is falling around us. Where will the birds go?
I think of all that's now gone, that's taken the *I*
that I was away from home, leaving only something

vague in my synapses and blood. Deep in the tree's
branches I found a nest. The salt trucks will open
the roads. Tomorrow we will make soup, likely
with what's left of the vegetables, blend them

with a can of chicken stock. Last night I read
that astronomers are all but sure there is
another planet in our solar system. Stillness
lies in the cat asleep on the hearth—a word

I love. The stillness may move into the air
around us, a quiet poignancy within our
own fragile and willing breath. I wonder
why I keep at the window, staring at the storm.

Feeding the Pup in the Early Morning

I love our pup, she whose DNA chooses to chew
the coffee table's legs, any book, shoe, or the pair
of reading glasses I left where anyone my age

would set them in case of fire, storm, the need
to finally pay a bill, much less an inappropriate
drop-in by someone you would never add to

your daughter's wedding invitation list. However,
it's 7 a.m. and I must feed her. There's a schedule,
a set of behaviors prescribed in validated tomes

by those who decided never to major in philosophy,
dance history, or literature. They opened their minds
to trial and error, determining a schedule is for sure

the only way to raise a confident and willing companion
who will on some unfathomable day give up dragging
anything dangling—bedspread, sweater, scarf, shower curtain—

who will come when called, sit, lie down, heel, fetch, love
me even when there is no treat. But it's 7 a.m. and I
staggered to bed after meeting a deadline at 3.

The schedule proclaims, "Feed the pup at the same time
every day." If she sleeps just a measly hour longer, do I
risk her turning into the neighborhood's teeth-baring

dingo who digs up Mrs. Phelps's petunias, snarls
at the priest on his daily walk, steals the dump truck
from the sandbox down the street, snaps at the kid

selling magazines for a trip to Haiti? Will I be
the one whose best friend must be muzzled just for
sleeping into just one more hour of just another day?

Do I take a rabid risk? Oh hell. Bless the kibble.

The Mallards

Yesterday I sat outside a cafe with
a cup of coffee and an acquaintance

who wanted to know if his poem
was any good. After reading it I

looked up and saw a male and a
female mallard waddling down

the walk. She stopped at a puddle
and drank. Then they sat at the edge

of the sidewalk. I watched them
as a man walked by, too close,

and they rose, then settled
themselves on the curb. They

were far from any water.
"Sure," I said. "It's good."

Thinking Again of My Daughter

Tonight the clouds moved on, and the stars lay
flat against the sky's black backdrop. The moon

sat full beneath Jupiter's deceptive white glow,
and Orion seemed to be falling headfirst toward

some anonymous emptiness. I sat on the couch,
skimming across television's landscape, tapping

the remote like some anachronistic telegraph
operator. Flicking into the past, I saw her

watching walruses heaving their inopportune
selves onto a shoal of ice, Bugs Bunny thumbing

his twitching nose at Elmer Fudd's exasperated
lack of R's, music videos, *Sesame Street,* even

the news and the History Channel. I paused
to watch an evangelist, became as mesmerized

as she did when she first saw Mr. Rogers. I
watched his hands, how they were able to point,

to lift themselves like dumb birds toward only
the roof. I thought how my father had always

pulled my hands out of my pockets, how even
today they feel strangely vulnerable hanging

at my sides. You had lunch today with your
granddaughter. You had a salad and some

pasta. You had dessert. You took her home.
When the news comes on tonight, I'll watch,

knowing tomorrow night the stars will have
moved. And in the morning, I will walk

the dog, trying not to pull him away when
he stops, fixes his nose on a clump of leaves.

The Nonattachment of Buddhism

My Aunt Dot would laugh
when she saw her shadow.
"Take it off! Take it off!"

Once a week we walked
the sidewalks of her little town—
boutiques, fancy jewelry store,

markets: one for meat, one
for fruit and vegetables, a quiet
bookstore—to the gray stone

library where the air carried
the welcoming smell of words.
I would take a book, tug out

the card from its pocket, and
when seeing only a name or two
wonder what it was like to be

something no one really cared about.
"Take it off!" my Aunt Dot laughed,
looking behind her as we headed home,

the sun turning its way down
and I tilting toward why she
didn't want to be with her loyal,

silent, unassuming silhouette.

My Brother—A Star

My mother was pregnant through the first
nine games of the season. We were 7-2.
I waited for a brother. My father
kept to the hard schedule. Waking
the morning of the tenth game, I thought
of skipping school and shooting hoops.
My cornflakes were ready, soggy. There
was a note: "The baby may come today.
Get your haircut." We were into January,
and the long December snow had turned
to slush. The wind was mean. My father
was gone. I looked in on my mother still
asleep, and hoped she'd be okay.
I watched her, dreamed her dream: John
at forward, me at guard. He'd
learn fast. At noon, my father
picked me up at the playground. My team
was ahead by six.
We drove toward the gym.
"Mom's okay," he said and tapped his fist
against my leg. The Plymouth ship that rode
the hood pulled us down the street.
"The baby died," he said. I felt my feet press hard
against the floorboard. I put my elbow on the door handle,
my head on my hand, and watched the town:
Kenner's Five and Ten, Walker's Hardware,
Jarret's Bakery, Shaffer's Barbershop, the bank.
Dick Green and Carl Stacey waved. "It was
a boy."
        We drove back to school. "You gonna
coach tonight?" "Yes." "Mom's okay?"
"Yes. She's fine. Sad. But fine. She said
for you to grab a sandwich after school. I'll see you
at the game. Don't forget about your hair." I

got out, walked in late to class.
"We're doing geography," Mrs. Wilson said. "Page
97. The prairie."
                      That night in bed
I watched this kid firing in jump shots
from everywhere on the court. He'd cut left,
I'd feed him a fine pass, he'd hit.
I'd dribble down the side, spot him in the corner, thread
the ball through a crowd to his soft hands, and he'd
loft a star up into the lights where it would pause
then gently drop, fall through the cheers and through the net.
The game never ended. I fell into sleep. My hair
was short. We were 8 and 2.

                             for my mother and my father

The Book of Rain

The Book of Rain sits, well, it can't really sit,
on the floor beside this chair where I also
sit, but this isn't really a chair; it's the daybed

my grandmother had and never used after
her husband died four months before I
was born. It had been snowing all day,

well, actually all night and then into the day.
From then on, she sat only on chairs, lay
only on his side of the bed. She had one

chair by "her window," another on the
porch where in good weather she smoked
and watched those walking by. I need

to open The Book of Rain and watch
photographs of rain-heavy clouds,
torrents and trickles, devastated homes

and flooded streets, puddles, kids just
standing in a daylight rain, night rain,
rivulets, people ducking under cover,

soaked dogs sitting at front doors.

The Day After William Stafford Died

There was to be a storm
and the rain came, but

the warning for severe weather
blinked off the lower-left corner

of the television just before 11.
The rain did last into the next morning,

a steady light fall that left
the gardens deeply watered

and the August heat less hot.
After it stopped, somewhere close

to noon, our dog and I walked
down to the lake. I stood where he

had stood, in his steady way.
Our dog did what she always does,

stepped into the water, then ran back
out and sniffed along the shore for fish.

The Line

Seventy-five years ago my mother and father got engaged

There is no need to know the date.
April is enough. Two years later,
my mother lay alone and I was

born and my father lay on his cot
in Belgium, or was it France? No, he
was being shipped to the Philippines,

lying in a hammock, sick. We are all
standing in line. The spaces between
us like those between these words.

When he came home, I was two. I
pointed at him and said, "Dada."
April's not that cruel. There are

daffodils. Pansies' antique blooms
hold through any cold. The line
we are in moves forward. It is

giving to receive a handout: bread,
a hat, shoes, even a book. Then he took
her hand, slipped a ring onto her finger.

It was quiet. She told me. There was a
breeze; in April there is always a breeze.
There was also a war. Two months later,

she began reading the front page, began
listening to the radio. It's difficult to know
anyone else in a line except the people

behind and in front of you. Today she
keeps a vase of dried milkweed pods and
gray-brown grasses on her kitchen table.

There are many lines. Some are very long.
Sometimes we forget we are standing there.
Then a tap on the shoulder and a nod to move ahead.

After the Thirteenth Shock Treatment

I asked for two fried egg sandwiches
and a blueberry milkshake. I got soup.
And it was raining, so instead of trying
again to read *Middlemarch,*

I lay on my side and watched the rain
glide down the window. I used to love
to go outside. My sister was a high school
cheerleader, someone everyone loved

to be around—if anything was good,
it was great. I needed to know. My God
spoke only in doubt. The nerves at the ends
of my fingers never slept, and when my fists

bloodied my forehead, only the comfort
of bandages let me look out across
the parking lot, out over the vans, Audis,
and pickups into the trees where I could

see how the leaves held to the limbs.
At home my father stayed alone in his
gardens. My mother carried her knitting
to a neighbor's and talked about dinner.

for Rebecca Klott

The Train Home

I imagined snow drifting down on the village, the skaters
tall on the little mirror that was my ice, and onto the train
that traveled the oval tracks, the watchman coming out

just before the engine passed the station—every
time, on time, in time and I left time itself upstairs
in the angry kitchen where the pans stacked

eight high came clattering down the stairs
without a signal for the engineer to brake. I
built a papier-mâché mountain, cast the news

into the paste and glued cotton over the headlines
turning the ubiquity of cruel into twisting
runs and unexpected moguls for the tin downhillers.

The Plasticville houses, stores, church,
and school held quiet safe. There were no
slaps that knotted a neck or raised a welt.

At the edge of town, a few inches beyond
the "Come Back Soon" sign, a lumberyard
offered jobs and a way to close each day

with what was on the radio: a symphony,
comic episode, detective serial. Upstairs
the world remained as unpredictable as

the common cold. But in the basement
the toys were real and never thought
I wasn't. I had a house in their village,

a church with a kind god, a school where I
could name the stars. When the sneer laughed
at my waste of time, I tapped on sleep's door,

welcomed by a pillow and another night.

I Almost Saw a Rabbit Today

He was wearing a Boursin homburg hat
and the sky was coated in blue after a night,
clear, dappled with stars, a crescent moon's

arc all but rocking slowly under Venus's
modest vigil. He looked at me. I waved.
Then the angels, four of them, got up and

walked from the porch, picked up
the horseshoes and began a game.
It was quiet, silent really, silent as

the stars' light, except for the ring
of the clink after each angel's fling,
one horseshoe after another clinging

to the rusty iron stakes. The rabbit
sat up, watched a dozen tosses, then
hopped on, none of us thinking

it wise or kind to follow. When one
of the angels missed, the game ended,
and back on the porch we talked it over.

Self-Pity as an Ars Poetica

They just keep coming,
saying, "Sorry to say no."
"We regret that these do
not meet our needs." "Your
party's simply not the kind
that we enjoy. We don't like
the games you play, your choice
of music, wine, those greasy
sausage balls stuck on a toothpick."

I'm a loser in the poetry
casino: I drop my quarters
in the slot, get two peaches
and a prickly pear,
a cherry blossom, red
wheelbarrow, and a dulcimer.
My persona has an identity crisis.
My inner emperor has
no ice cream. I should have
been lying in a hammock
at anybody's farm. And now

I'm writing this beside
the stream behind our house,
my wife planting cosmos,
our dogs sleeping, their huge
heads snoring on their soft
paws, a robin feeding her
young, their necks stretching
from the nest in the branches
tangled above my head.

or D. L. James

Ice Storm

Here on the couch with my old dog I find
I'm feeling gratitude, an odd gratitude,
an old gratitude, one I thought had gone

for good down a long back road
that led away from the years when
I felt glad, felt what I believed

was an abiding gratitude: to be,
to be warm, and grateful to be
warm, to have some pillows

and a dozen books and all afternoon.
To be alone without even a sideswipe
of loneliness. To be on page 47,

or 114, or page 1 and there
was nothing missing. The ice
storm made things warm, time

irrelevant, made the sleeping
dog an amen to a prayer
never needing to be said.

Some of What Was Left After Therapy

The sky staying open to its stars and
the paradigm of ever-changing clouds.

Watching three boys playing catch
in a mown field of winter wheat.

Having the choice to sit on the porch
or deadhead the wilting blooms.
And of course adding one more
perennial, this time maybe coral bells.

To know:
The monks are asleep.
The monks are awake.
The monks are in prayer.
The monks may be walking their dogs.

A woman in a minivan stopping
as I was walking my dog.
"I lost my dog last week.
May I pet him? Her?"
Letting her pet him.

Still no answer for the ocean.

Xylem rises. Phloem falls.

Somewhere a man is buying a hat.
Somewhere a woman is buying a hat.

Turning to the Psalter

It's a quiet morning, time for matins, the sun
sending its preface through the maples' leaves.
My god is here, sitting beside me on the porch.

We're waiting for the day's new full light.
My god, of course, is not very well known
in eschatological circles. I call my god "God."

Just as I do each morning, God also watches
what comes into the space the eye creates. We
do this throughout the day, glancing out a window,

or on the way to whatever is on the list.
I like being religious in this unimportant way.
Just me and God worshipping by watching.

God's glad we can sit here or rake leaves or
clean the basement or listen to LeadBelly.
Yesterday I removed a dear friend from

the Rolodex. There in blue ink was his name
and his late wife's and his address for the past
eleven years. They will be staying here now.

I took a bit of time and looked at their names
and the grace of the record: thirty-four years
sending/receiving nonobligated holiday cards.

Before tossing the worn-down address into
the recycle bin, I showed it to God, who nodded,
took it, smiled, then led me outside to the back door

where God knelt and set it on the first step.

The Man Who
Decided to See

The Man Who Decided to See

And for the first time he saw
the boy whose bicycle sped by

his porch, then the yellowing leaf
on the back step. He saw a cloud bank

in his rearview mirror, and followed
the winding glide of the crack

in the sidewalk he took to the grocery
where he saw the woman in the bakery

look down, then touch her eye; the way
his wife's hair spread across her shoulders

in the photo on the top of the television,
the picture's frame chipped in the lower-left

corner. Stars; the moon; the scarred cutting board.
The way the light fell across their bed.

Dailiness

This morning after the angels had put on
their scarves and mittens and said their
good-byes and headed out into the surprise

of the first snow, he put away the recipe
for crepes, washed the plates, the other
dishes, silverware, put the butter in cold

water, and poured a second cup of coffee.
The moon was not yet set at 8:30, and it
made him remember how he never wanted

to leave his grandmother, her house, her
porch, her lap where she would read
to him, often a chapter from *Moby Dick*

or a comic—Felix the Cat, Buck Rogers—
an Uncle Wiggly story, something from
the King James Bible. Today he knew

what lay ahead: he would feed the fish
in his little pond, cut back what had died
in the flower bed, get pumpernickel bread

and orange marmalade, then the mail, maybe
stop at Jane's Depot and buy some new
warm socks. And he needed to decide

what book to read next. And what
to have tomorrow for breakfast when
the angels would be back around 7:30.

for Nancy Willard

The Last Days of Sam Snead

He stepped up to the first tee, the old master
of the Masters, tipped that classy straw hat,
waggled his faithful driver, took that easy
back swing, the one that had taken him cleanly
down every trip to the green, and hooked
his drive smack into the gallery of acolytes
sending their awe into the horror of disbelief.
Everything stilled: the azaleas gaudy
in their pinks, the caddies cleaning the clubs
of the next in line, the prim protectorate
of Old Augusta. Sam stood stunned for no
longer than a follow-through, apologized to
the worshipper who had taken the hit, shyly
took a drop, and hit a three iron out onto
the sloping grass, shuffled down the fairway,
eye fixed on the flag. This should have been
the last drive of a god, a slam from Olympus,
the ball starting out low, then rising into
the sweet southern air, lingering at its apogee
against the impossible Georgia sky, then landing
with a twitch of suspense just past the dreaded
edge of a yawning bunker, rolling another thirty
yards to a quiet stop in the center of the clean-cut
roll of the grass. No one knew this would
be Sam's last drive off a number one tee.
It's embarrassment that drives us out even
for a master who carried his clubs with grace,
always styling the perfect swing. Maybe
it came as a sigh of relief for all who had
stepped up to the tee, three foursomes waiting
to hit, all those who had taken a dozen practice
swings, shifted their weight until everything
felt just right, adjusted their grip one last time
and coming down into the ball had topped it,
sending it off like some buckshot-riddled rabbit
hopping down the fairway fifty yards at best.

After Learning a Literary Magazine's Editor Expects the First Line to Be a Grabber

Call Me Ishmael.
The rock band four blocks away sends
its Party-Till-the-Sun-Comes-Up beat

wrapped in aberrant guitar riffs onto the porch,
onto the porch where among the pots
nailed to the railing and trailing

creeping jenny down the slats I listen
and wonder just a bit, just for a moment,
where it all went, leaving me

here in the early September air.
The book I'm reading has no
main character. That's how it's been

for a while. Mostly we do our work,
look back for a second, recall when
we believed we'd gotten a good job,

look forward, knowing after thirty years
we didn't. What did we know? What
do we know now? I know the band

is rocking and that those there are likely dancing,
likely having a third or fourth drink, absolutely
sure they're having a really good time.

The Bird Maker

My husband loved
those shiny lawn
globes, how they'd

kick back the sun.
We had forty.
He wanted more.

He'd stare at them
for hours. I'd walk
around him; he'd

just keep staring.
I started carving
birds. I like wood.

He didn't. Once,
I set some birds
beside a couple

globes. He didn't
say a thing. He's
buried where I

don't want to be.

Levitating Frogs

[The frog] is supported by the force of magnetism.
      —Sir Michael Berry and Andre Geim, who caused
          a frog to levitate

Frogs should float on ponds, croak
over mats of algae, dive into
the dark brown of bottom mud.

But Sir Michael and Andre splayed
a frog on an electric current. It hovered,
spun above its tadpoles wriggling over rocks,

water bugs skimming across the light's long
gloss, above a single fly settling on
a wilting leaf away from the slurping reach

of the frog's unraveling tongue. Sir Michael
and Andre have videos: of the frog of course,
and of a single drop of water, and a strawberry,

each violating gravity. They imagine us
one day waking to peepers hanging
mid-jump on the morning air, a floating

world of teapots, spoons, candles, beds;
and rising on the air between here and
there—roses, lilies, Queen Anne's lace

blooming in a cottage garden planted
by Magritte while we, unmagnetized,
will stagger, stare into the heavens

terrified the evangelist on channel 2 was right.

It's What He Does Instead

Out here, the paint stays
between his fingers—a boat,

a long afternoon, this wide
and generous landscape. He

likes the smells: grass, yellow,
the insides of old hats, rain,

the rot of logs and leaves.
He wonders about church.

He'd like to paint the pews.
He likes every afternoon, how

the morning empties and opens,
and birds and light come into it,

how the color moves north or
veers into his neighbor's yard.

And he likes where his hand goes
when the brush takes it across

a board or broken dinner plate,
an old bedspring, shoes, those

tin trays over there beside
the bicycles, or these stumps.

When he's out here, it's quiet
and the wind settles on his hands.

Coffee Talks with Con Hilberry

He brought out the robust flavor
of everything, brewed us lines perked

for sipping, savoring—images
espresso intense, carried latte light

across rhythms energetic as caffeine.
We pour these poems—dark, rich,

some with cream, none with a sugar cube,
but each accompanied by the lonely sweetness

of a buttery croissant, one dipped
into the full body of a fine French roast.

                                        for Jane Hilberry

The Night Before the MLA, Casey Stengel Appears to the Postmodernist Theorists

"You ever take a pitch when the count's 3-1?
Slide home on a single to right? One time
the wind in Chicago threw my boys off.

Whitey was furious when I pulled him
with two out in the sixth, but you have to know
when to bring in your heat." The theorists open

their titanium briefcases, grab their Pilot pens
and spiral notebooks. This is the deconstruction
they've been hoping for. Casey waits, then

starts back up. "One Wednesday, a week after
my stomach quit achin', I told the boys, 'We
gotta shine our spikes and button our shirts.'

Mick and Moose said, 'Sure.' But Billy
overslid second. The bleachers were empty.
Tells ya somethin'." The theorists are dazed.

They ask him to explicate. "Sure, I'll explicate.
It's all about the home field advantage. Unless
Conlin was behind the plate. Then you might as well

go to a movie. If it's a night game, well now, that's
not the same, it's different. There's a difference.
Right, Yogi? Next year. Next year. Not last. Gotta

go, boys." The theorists say, "Thank you, Casey,"
shake his hand, have him sign their books, high-five
one another, and retreat to their hotel. They order

room service, change their panel to "Signs Don't
Have to Signify: Words, Ontology, and the Void
between Pitches." The Q & A lasts two hours.

The Week After

The boys, eight and seven,
have gone home with their father.
He will read to them tonight

for the first time, opening
to the page where there
is a bookmark

a lopsided elephant drawn
on it. Tomorrow he will learn
which son wants only

Rice Chex and which wants
nothing on his toast
but blueberry jam.

The Man Who Made Towers of Beach Glass

They reach green,
brown, blue, red,
and sunlight clear.
He never adds
a piece larger
than a half
dollar, is glad
when he sees
a head tilt back,
eyes staring up
into the refractions
of heaven. He
asks everyone
who stops by
if they know
about beach glass?
"Water rolls the edges
smooth, rounds
them so they won't
cut anything. Stand
here. Watch."

This American Walking the Winter Streets of Tübingen, Germany: A Postcard

The snow would fall in flakes so clear I would see their shapes, each,
as we know, singular before losing itself on the others, turning
number into amount, creating Brancusi mounds on porch rail mule posts,

small car hoods and rounded roofs, nineteenth-century lampposts; drifting
into solid and unbreaking waves; lying across the narrow curving
streets and alleyways, along the plane tree branches drooping over

the sidewalks; sliding down the sledding hills; slanting like danger down
the steep roof of each pale-painted home: yellow, blue, brown, mauve, all
adjoined at the side walls, stucco to stucco blending into one another;

front windows upstairs and down, broad frames foregrounded and drawing
my eye to dawn-soft light tempering wall-lined bookshelves, shelf after
shelf of painted platters, plates, cups, tureens, and teapots. On the piano

glimpsed in the corner a thoughtfully haphazard flock of family photos:
uncombed children, aunts, grandparents, all of them staring ahead, some
laughing, some caught stern. I would walk into the silence which is not

an absence of anything that matters, with the good company of stillness,
the moon far away, the light lost in an eternity of blue sky, a neighbor
shoveling his walk, a pot of coffee inside with his old wool blanket.

for Norbert Kraas

Saint Peter and the Goldfinch

He'd filled the little-roofed feeders with
sunflower and thistle seeds, hooks hanging
sturdy from the birch's branches twisting

his own arm's length above the mulch path,
the day's first light lapsing along the leaves.
Peter knew the neighbors were talking

about the guy in the frayed cassock
who last week moved in with only
a pickup's bed of what seemed to be

belongings—a small table, couple
of ladder-back chairs, a sound system
that looked vintage, a lot of books,

three futons, a large canvas bag
maybe filled with pans, pots, dishes,
and three lamps, one that dangled

tiny stars from its frayed shade.
He had gone out and brought home
an Adirondack and about fifty flower pots,

and the feeders. Now he took his morning
green tea out to the chair to wait for the birds.
This, he felt cross his mind, is what I have

waited for. He sipped. A house finch came.
A couple cardinals, a downy woodpecker.
The chickadees would take a seed, fly

into the branches of the hemlocks surrounding
the house, and batter to get to the meat. Time
and time again they returned. Peter tried

to count then wondered why, stopped
and thought about what to plant
in the pots, where he would place them

within the striped grass that made a nest
for the house to sit within. He liked thinking
he had nested. He liked thinking everything

here could be taken away. He had cosmos,
impatiens—no perennial until bloom
and loss became a ritual, sacred. There was

a breeze. There was the tea. And then there was
a goldfinch, just one, at the thistle feeder, its startle
of yellow and black seamless within its feathers.

Peter watched as it took the seed, sat above him.
He watched as the bird flew to the feeder, flew back
to the same branch. Saint Peter and the goldfinch

here in the day's beginning. He could not bow
his head. He knew joy's coupled sorrow. He knew
that this was time. He knew what the earth knew.

Watching

Clouds, of course, are the greatest things
                in the world: cumulus,   cirrus,
nimbus,   you   name it. How they
arrive
                        out of nowhere, it seems,   coast
        across the sky's scrim, some thin and
wispy as milkweed seed, some
                                seemingly stuffed with down, great
pillows for God's huge and heavy head.
        These are, of course, the benevolent ones.
Even at night we know they are passing

                                silently above us
as if some kindly neighbor has come out in the cold to pull the comforter up
to our chin.   Of course,
        there are the grays, carriers of uncertainty: holding perhaps
rain or sleet, snow or hail, or not a drop of anything at all. We can
                never know.

        Then, of course, the dark and bleak lugging a foreboding storm,
clouds
    that send us under cover, into resigned and
listless
                                listening to the chaos on the roof,
the slash   across the car's front window,
wipers all but useless against the tipping of some cosmic water barrel.
But then   again, of course,
                            no matter what the cause,
what the effect.
                we just might see any cloud—
                                            eerie dark,
        marshmallow white,
erasure gray—

                become an old man's hat, a Conestoga wagon,
    hippopotamus,
                the face of Aunt Louise.

Packing the Boxes

He was thinking about the way
the moon's light fell across
the porch, how the days

seemed to pile or drift until
the garden began to show
itself again. So he dragged

out the boxes he'd tossed
into the basement. He packed
them with all the things he'd

found, gathered, brought home
from his daily walks. All year
he'd sifted through piles of stuff,

along curbs, behind stores, left
after a flea market, or stacked
with a "Take it, it's yours" sign.

One of the best spots was outside
the art room at the grade school.
Every week he collected what

the students didn't want. Some
of the boxes he filled. In others,
he put one thing—an old

Christmas ornament, finger
painting, letter, toy tugboat—
then filled the rest with paper.

He packed for days, often eating
breakfast in the afternoon, never
answering the phone. He

taped them shut, then painted them,
covering each with dots and swirling
lines, splashes and drips, a tree,

a cow, a sun and moon and stars, and
then one tiny house with a high-pitched
roof; blue, red, or yellow smoke rising

in a slim line from a crumbling stone chimney.

Heaven

Groucho guards the gate, more
bewildering than God in judging
supplicants. Behind him Harpo,

his hair reason enough to realize
there's nothing we can do. "Say
the secret word." "Logos!"

we shout. Groucho taps his long
cigar. "What?" he laughs. "Logos?!
What the hell is logos?" We

are terrified. We look to Harpo.
He smiles, shrugs, honks his horn,
pulls some celery from his coat

and gnaws. Groucho lights
a new cigar, arcs his eyebrows,
moving the clouds of heaven higher,

then looks so sadly at us that we ache
to know what we have done. Groucho
turns his back, catches sight of a slithery

blonde and slinks his way away,
healing the sullen, turning loaves
and fishes into parakeets, and

somehow dragging us through
into the madness of eternity.

Rising over the Smoke

She wonders what dream
will come next, will slip up
her back and carry her out
into the pile of wood. She

pulls her hat down over her ears,
wondering how she'll fix another
angel to the side of the house, let it
hover there over the window. Now

it's time. The cats want in. She wants
out. She carries her sack of nails,
her hammer, the one her grandfather
used to build the house that burned

the night she was born. She saw
her mother rise over the smoke,
float off over the stand of pines.
She reaches into the pile, pulls

out a dozen pieces of maple, grabs
a dozen more pieces. She gets
the buckets of red, blue, and
yellow and paints the boards,

the snow freezing over
her hair, melting into
the paint; the wind howling
across each painted board.

The World in May Is Leafing Out

It's Matisse on a bicycle. It's
a great blue heron coloring
outside the lines. The show's
turned over to the aftermath
of buds. You can love
never thinking
this cliché could turn
to ice. Even nice
can be profound
as worry, even
the creek over the rotting log,
the pansy in the moss-covered
pot. The birds bulge
with song. Mary Cassatt
throws open her windows.
Monet drags his pallet,
sits and waits for the paint
to spill across the patina
of his failing sight. Erik Satie
makes his joyous cling
and clang a counterpoint
to dazzle. The earth is rising
in shoots and sprays.
The sky's as new as rain.
The stubborn doors swing open.

Chamber Musicians Also Wash the Dishes, Check the Mail

But now the chamber musicians are
just past halfway in Glazunov's Elegie,

the part where in rehearsal they stopped.
"It feels as if I'm behind." "I don't think

so. I think I'm ahead." When I listened
all I heard was a whole note held

in the third movement of a symphony
by Tinnitus, all I felt was the wax waning

onto the timpani of my eardrum.
Next comes another elegy, this by Suk,

Suk who was fifteen when he wrote its
sorrow-filled walk through what he did

not yet know. The chamber musicians
know. They carry elegy in their fingers.

They open the world on the other side
of every note and let us breathe

within the haunting space between each
touch of key and pull of bow. They believe

heaven is between the stars, music
in the empty sleeve of the one-armed man.

He of the Long Wait

Every morning he invited the wind
into his open window. Then he would lean
out and, believing the trees were listening,

would whisper, "Welcome back." He
wanted the weeds to nod, for the birds
to carry his breathing to their nests.

In the afternoon he sat in the theater
of sparrows, juncos, nuthatches
under the loft and languid passing

of clouds and imagined applauding
the man two doors down who walked
by with his three dogs. He loved

the ubiquity of time. In his basement
he had a puppet stage painted pale blue
with a crimson curtain where each night

the puppets—a rabbit in a beret, a mole
with a walking stick, a man with a beard
full of nettles, and a woman holding

a golden basket of pears—talked about
their day. Then he went to sleep, the sky
deepening behind the ceiling of stars.

The Long Married

Suite for Another Day in the World

I

Everything Bloomed Earlier This Year

While another fissure cut
off another wall of ice,

all the earth's water rising,
our magnolias, lilacs, redbuds,
azaleas lifted

their color into the sun
and tonight's forecast—
frost.

We will cover the forget-me-nots

and the cluster of peonies
her grandmother
first planted
in her hidden garden.

We'll drape
a sheet over the haphazard
assemblage of crocuses, daffodils, and jonquils.

The lily of the valley's sprawl
will hold

against the cold.

In the basement,
where it's just warm enough,
the spiders will hang their webs.

II

The Snow Has Been Gone a Week

The sky is a scrim
behind the dark-barked
trees, their branches

waiting in the negative
space of air. This light
lingers in the stark

limbs, along the way
of spring's occasion
of crocus and violet. I

think feathers, abandoned
nests, letters with no
envelopes, and a new lamp.

On the counter beneath
the kitchen window
the cat sleeps curled

into herself, parenthetical
between this melt
and April's onion snow.

III

Sparrow

I have no idea if you are lark,
java, white-throated, vesper,
song, or saltmarsh sharp-tailed.

I have Sibley's guide, Peterson's,
and one for our area. But even if
I memorized your markings,

you would not be the bird sitting
on the lowest branch of the old beech
outside our bedroom window. I want

to cross this space into the world
you know: the branches where you perch,
the ground where you search, the air . . .

IV

Again the Squirrels

The squirrels are hanging
from the feeder meant
for the morning
arrival of grosbeaks, finches,

chickadees, the assertive
jays. The feeder clangs,
dangling,
and I try to sit
zazen, feel

the startled
beat
of my silly heart
wanting to slam
the door
sending
black tails, gray tails
sailing

from their clutch
of the ebony, oiled sunflower seeds.
"Only for the birds," I chant. "Only
for the birds," my mantra mocking
myself, my morning, my

monotonous hope
that the day will unfold into
something other
than its inevitable
chatter, its necessary way
of forcing us
to interrupt.

I will wait

for night,
for the moon's light
draping across our eyes, for

a rainfall that mutes it all.

V

Maybe

It's another morning, the sun
pulled slowly hand over hand

to sow its earth-bound light
dappling the grasses,

fuzzy whites, lady's mantle,
lamb's ear, and lying across

the variegated leaves, hexing
what we think we see. Beside

the lily-padded pond, the frogs
with ever-croaking gulp swallow

the light's arrival. On the porch
the dog at peace between his paws.

VI

The View from the Porch

The gray squirrel takes its circular
route up the maple, out on a limb, leaps

to a branch on the white pine, onto
the curly willow, back down and

around the trunk, stops to scratch,
then heads across the garden.

A red-winged blackbird balances
on the top of the pink azalea,

its last blooms landing amid
the swatch of maidenhair ferns.

The hostas are rising, their leaves
green and blue-green and widening

as if receptive to any ant or rain.
My grandmother spent fifty-three

years on the porch, in her chair—
a pot of tea, biscuits, currant

jam, her Pall Malls, and a fresh
deck of cards to fill her day

with solitaire. She talked to
herself as if collecting those

who walked by. "Will she ever
get rid of that hat?" "It's Wednesday

so there's lousy liquor in his bag."
Our pansies are getting leggy.

The shaggy irises are blossoming.

VII

The Cat and I Watch the Morning

It's what we do. Each morning.
The cat still sleeping on the sill, tail

twitching. Standing at the window,
I sip my coffee, new-brewed and

caramel-creamed. Within the sprawl
of this light, I want to turn and say,

"Watch how the light moves across
the liriope, sharp-cutting in shafts

through the winter leftovers of
brown and yellow, how it lies

on the platter-leaved butterbur,
drips down the fragile dangle

of coral bells and columbine, settles
into the full dark of the hemlock."

VIII

Stopping at the Window to Watch the Squirrels

It is early Monday morning and it is
gray. And it is January, a gray early
Monday in January. There is snow

on our borrowed bit of earth.
Most everyone is working or
going to work or coming home. Out

the backyard window, through
the stagger
of hemlocks, blue spruce,
and white pines, the juncos,
wrens, finches, redpolls,
nuthatches, and chickadees rise

and dive like lost kites on
a wind-filled day, then dart
within the tangles
of branches
to the feeders hanging,
perhaps
high enough, perhaps
low enough,

a sprawl of dropped black-oil sunflower seeds
dappled among the fallen pine cones. We
no longer go to work. We keep
the feeders full and fill
our cups with coffee,

hot and tempered with cream.

The Inevitable Sorrow
of Potatoes

Halfway into the ubiquitous diminishment
that is Vermeer's November, we know
the chill while the juncos, chickadees,

a downy woodpecker, and the ever
upside-down nuthatch all cling
to the feeder. In mid-June we turned

over our sun-spotted plot and settled
what would be golden-brown potatoes
into the company of worms and along

the bypass of moles. We believe in
the modesty of potatoes, the humble
spuds that carry the legacy of famine.

There can be no knowing if things can
molder deep, if a blight can singe
the mottled skins: scarring variations

on the darkening silence that too soon
will shorten the dog's walk into pause
and sniff, a few steps more to another

sniff and then back home. A cardinal
is taking fallen sunflower seeds
back to his mate, head cocked

in the hemlock. One night we surprised
ourselves talking about potatoes, their
stark humility, how they offer to the sanguine

1 percent an au gratin choice, to the hungry
a skin with a slap of butter. Last month
we sent our spades into their patch, carved

them out from the summered earth.
Their skins had blackened, marred
by what we could not know was there.

for Rosemerry Wahtola Trommer

Key West Suite

I

Flying in over the Gulf

Maybe the clear water leads me to believe
coral is God's last hiding place.
But it's likely just the end of the highway,

the way U.S. 1 stitches the islands
and tethers them to the bony finger
of the mainland. Something

makes me feel some of it will last:
a tin roof, the wood of a lobster trap,
bougainvillea winding through a wire fence.

The plane comes down across the haphazard flyway
of pelicans. An egret waits, motionless
beside a fishing boat rocking against a canal wall.

Tonight we will go out and look for osprey
in the mangroves, Key deer in the scrub pines.
We will feel them trusting us, then go home.

Then after we hang up our binoculars,
I'll go to Arnie's Seawater Shop and buy
us one of those pieces of pink coral,

the kind with a phony blue dolphin
rising up behind a seashell, just a bit
of yellow glue showing along the edge.

II

Another Day

Our houseboat is a little houseboat.
Some are two stories, three

bedrooms, a roof-top patio garden,
the view taking the eye across

the bight out over the cypress
and onto the Gulf where the tarpon

slow dance and the fishing boats
settle in, lines tossed or dropped.

Those on vacation can rent a charter
and hope to take home a photograph

of their catch, the tough-scaled fish,
having fought and given in, now hanging

alongside the smiles. Today again
the clouds will pass over us,

the sun will bring sliding light
across the water, time will bring

its illusion to carve its way
into our ephemeral cells,

and we will sit again on our deck,
the wind chime alchemizing the breeze.

III

Overcast on the Island

The tarpon lie laconic alongside
our little house, their fins slowly

fanning to keep them in place. We
too move in place, letting the boat

welcome the low-knot breeze
as it rocks us gentle into the gray

day's opening. We have little other
than coffee brewed strong against

the scrim of dispiriting news.
The island's one seaplane slides

onto the ocean's runway as fighter jets
outdistance their roar, straight-lining

their terrible glide back to base.
The gulls hover, coast, turn, swerve

against, into, and on the updraft, laughing
as they lurk above the open-wide bight.

Across my sight, houseboats sit steady
against the pier, each rocking within

the sun's filtered rise, inhabitants here
all but anonymous in their unencumbered

ways of getting by. Soon our dog will open
one eye, yawn, lay his head back down.

Rain is the dogma of the day. We have
our coffee, each other nothing but each other.

IV

The Tourists' Last Day

is always much like the others: sirens,
planes bringing in the next gaggle
of one-week visitors hoping to feel

tropical, to be who they can't be at home.
They will have to narrow down the places
to dine, drink, and even get so loaded

they couldn't care if the wind takes them past
the last stop. They won't make their beds,
will find their way to breakfast, think

they've felt the sloppy ghost of Hemingway
at Captain Tony's when all they have is a

T-shirt and a photo of a six-toed cat. Does it

matter? After all, Hem made it up too. They
will hear the music dissonantly merging
on Duval, tell everyone back home that they

heard it "the way it's supposed to be played."
Maybe they'll take a charter out to where
dropping a line is like grabbing a floating

duck at the carnival. Maybe they will snorkel,
the salt they swallow later rising as a briny
memory within a parched and peeling skin.

V

Listening to Baseball on the Back of the Boat

The Pirates are up 2–0 in the bottom of the fifth.
An hour ago, I watched a rehabbed houseboat
being towed across the bight and into its slip,

the owners Pittsburghers who wandered down
into the sun and humidity of Key West. The water's
dappled oblongs of light ripple laconically and

the sky is all but gull-less. Tonight the saved
boat's owners will couple again—perhaps—
the same sun setting its lower light through

their new windows. Now it's the seventh inning.
I don't know why I'm listening. Maybe I am
twelve. And maybe they are seventeen again,

finding themselves in an old new boat, surprised
that this saving has maybe salvaged a twitch
of themselves even though never in the plans.

A Dodger just homered with two on,
making it 3–2. Looking back across the water,
I watch four cormorants dive, surface, dive.

VI

Blue Sky over the Bight

Sometimes when we stand in the loss
of it all, surrounded by what we will never

be, the sky seems to be just fine. It's blue.
It's many shades of blue. And it's there

and will be when we join the landscape
of the invisible. Clouds cross, none ever

the same. And that's when we realize again
that there actually is no sky, just another

anonymous unknown we are sure we see.
When our dog steps out onto the deck of

our little houseboat bobbing on the nameless
blue-green of this bight and lifts his nose into

the gull-crossed and sea-soaked breeze,
does he see our sky? I like to suppose

he does. Though most likely it's something
his gentle nose has brought for only him.

Remembering the Night I Dreamed Paul Klee Married the Sky

We went out for dinner, down
some lackadaisical alley, threading
our way among leftover handshakes, sleeping

former aristocrats, and scattered scraps
of newsprint still holding words against
the wind. Above us, the old sky held

its cross-stitch of stars and we half expected
the light to shiver in our back pockets.
It was just that we knew. It was

just that it was cold. In the window
of the Italian restaurant, we saw a couple,
likely in their sixties, looking at each other.

She dipped her bread into her soup
while he drank his wine. Then she reached
across the table, took his hand, and lay

a spoon across his palm. We went in. I
remember how big the napkins were.

Let It Snow

She wants to sleep. Oh, how she wants to sleep.
Till 9, 10, please, till noon a dream, a hope.
She knows the snows are piling dark and deep
and she has promises to keep and cope
with after miles and miles to drive instead
of sleep. She shakes the harness from her eyes,
heaves up her snuggled self from her warm bed,
pulls on wool, sighs to face the snow's surprise.
She grabs the shovel, makes her snow-blown way
from front-door step by shoveled step to get
to where the antique plow man peers, this day
waiting, bill in hand. Now she's wool-soaked wet
and muscle-sore. Her spirit's nearly leveled,
she's distraught, dis-shoveled, and disheveled.

Suite for the Long Married

I

The Long Married

We wake at differing times, the old
dog even later. I make the coffee

the night before, set the time
for it to perk. We ready ourselves

for the day, all the usual, never
nervous about our hair, what shoes

to wear, often leave on the socks
we slept in, our hands linked into

the loss of night. We do a lot of
waiting—for calls from family,

for the dog to pee, in line for most
everything we need, which isn't much.

The bins of wants are full, and yet
we want to want, and so we go

to the antique mall, garage sales, now
and then a local church bazaar. "Just

looking" is our common conversation
as we wander from shop to gallery,

thing to thing, post office box
to pharmacy. No longer needing

a reason to live, we let ourselves be.
Better this way: giving a damn or not.

II

Solstice After All These Years

The work days go unnoticed.
It's always a truck load;
it's always maybe, or

another hour. Last night
we watched as the possum
crossed the backyard, padding

its small path back into
the ineffable chaos
of wood and molder.

This morning there will be
a cup of coffee. There
will be the fierce pull

of the news' hypnosis.
We will try not to remember.
We will tug ourselves to the novel

we roamed with into the anonymity
of sleep. We will be religious
without faith or doubt.

The trees will be our amen.
The cedar waxwing at the feeder
will take our place at Communion,

redeeming seed into flight and song.
Tonight within the moon's generosity
we will gather the vestments for tomorrow.

III

Morning with Dogs

The old dog won't get up. The pup
is yelping. We want to sleep another

hour, half an hour, fifteen minutes.
We are old dogs, too.

But the pup is hungry and the light
is crossing the evergreens and now

that we have found our way out of bed
and on to the dogs' bowls, the old dog's

eyes open. The coffee—timed when
to perk—is dripping through the grounds.

And though wanting still to sleep, we
divide the morning's rituals: filling

the feeders for the rampant demands
of chickadees, finches, the one downy;

letting the old dog out first to pee
unencumbered by the pup's romping

plea to play. This is the opening of our
every day. And we go on, the past

always tugging us back into regret.

IV

Poem Beginning with "Of Course"

Of course there are days when
the story slowly becomes one
we have known before: quiet

except for the highway
humming a mile away
while we still sleep within

the dream that hasn't yet
awakened us. The morning
will slip away like the dew

on the hostas, ferns, and
butterbur. Midafternoon
will hang its heavy heat

on the spiders' webs
while the cosmos droop
their startle of pink into

the bees' bypass. Our ragged
cushions sit on the haphazard
disassembly of Adirondacks

we bought when we wondered
if we would stay where time
now settles into itself, the two

of us waiting within what lingers.

V

When a Quiet Comes

Sometimes when the morning surrounds 7 a.m.,
a quiet comes. A neighbor wakes, lets out
the dog, fills the songbird feeder. Often

a jogger goes by. Mostly there is the quiet.
There is a pot of coffee. Here in this house
there is a cat who seems to take the day's

oncoming disappointments and hold them
in her purr. The mind almost shuts down.
The garden's tapestry of buds and blooms

waits for not a thing. There is this quiet,
this way the day has of being where
we belong. At precisely 7:45 the bells

of Saint Peter's will send an old hymn into
the quiet and we who are still pilgrims
will then walk our way into another day.

VI

Can We Know?

Our old dog's been sleeping
most of the day, breathing heavily.

We say, "Well, he's old. Maybe
that's all it is." We think we know

him. He barks when it's time
for his walk or when he needs

to pee. Did he alchemize from
abandonment into one of us

because of how he looks at us,
because of the biscuits, because

of all the smells in the backyard?
Damn anyone who calls us

sentimental. We believe in
the comfort of his wag, his

lying every night amid our
long and given marriage.

No one asks for loneliness.

VII

Sometimes in the Early Morning the Losses Come

They sit here,
each one waiting
for another

to finish
her story, his story.
Maybe they need

to tell them again. Maybe
they want me
to listen, then

take them
into the garden
where they will carry

their ubiquity of quiet
among the early
bloom of lupine,

gay feather, and the peonies
that have offered
their frazzled globes

into forty years.
The goat's beard spreads
its extravagance of off-white

on the mute rug
of moss, the twisting
branches of curly willow

draping over the dangling
dazzle of the golden chain.
Everything is rising from

the earth's dark silence,
the losses walking with us
into the labyrinth of day.

VIII

Love Poem

The smaller the talk the better.
I want to sit with you and have us
Solemnly delight in dust; and one violet;
And our fourth night out;
And buttonholes. I want us
To spend hours counting dog hairs,
And looking up who hit .240
In each of the last ten years.
I want to talk about the weather;
And detergents; and carburetors;
And debate which pie our mothers made
The best. I want us to shrivel
Into nuthatches, realize the metaphysics
Of crossword puzzles, wait for the next
Sports season, and turn into sleep
Holding each other's favorite flower,
Day, color, record, playing card.
When we wake, I want us to begin again
Never saying anything more lovely than garage door.

IX

What Holds

Now we say, "There's always the coffee."
And there's the dog we call "Spare Parts."

He's twelve, our fourth, our marriage
held by each dog who's lain beside us.

We do not know how old we are.
We are resting on the earth.

Today downtown there is an opening
at a gallery, and in the heart of the garden

the lupines' hues are rising along
the quieting strength of their stems.

It is early, the sun rising behind
the quilt of cloud that has comforted

us through the night. And there's enough
coffee for two more cups, one with cream.

Here

When morning
falls
across the sparrow

on the stump
and the cat sleeps on
the sill,

and when last year
comes
to mind,

and when we
come back
from traveling deep

in our sleep, and
our daughter
returns

to the way
she says,
"Hello,"

we will sit here
watching
the leaves dropping

onto the creek,
moving on the quiet
of the leaf-strained light.

Waiting for the Astronomer

Practicing Chinese
Ink Drawing

Outside this window
the trees
are black-branched,
covered
by an overnight
fall of snow.
Everything is still,
no wind,
no wind on its way,

and the sky—deep
blue, vague
behind a gray
scrim, mimics
the stillness
of this snow
while
my brush strokes
carry the feel
of listless
luck—languid
and precise
as the single file
the toms tracked
this morning
into the woods
whose branches
and snow
and light
cannot be drawn.

The Question of Prayer

Monks know we can be one
with the world without words,

a name, not even a murmur
or breath. Within the modesty

of presence prayer could be green,
slow, tattered, cold, alone

as a possum crossing
a back road. It's the touch

of the still. It's where
we are Amen, Shalom,

Namaste—it's our there, here,
our forgotten habitat of yes.

We become sigh, our "I"
the wet dog, the sparrow nesting

in the anonymity of brown.

for Randy Smitt

Nearing November

Here in this room there are chairs,
an old radio, a table covered with

maps. The lamp tilts away from
the window, its light falling across

the maps. In this room there is a
wooden sculpture, one shape now

lost to another. Looking out into
the sky, I think star, the infinite

riff of atom, the endless solo of form.

Waiting for the Astronomer

We live in a universe of patterns. Every
night the stars move in circles across
the sky.
—Ian Stewart, *Nature's Numbers*

I want time's run-on sentence.

I want to draw an unassuming
teleological line from one star
to any other, hoping the silent

trace of light will mark
our walk away. An astronomer
can measure the negative space

between each star, the absence
of light within the extravagance
of a galaxy's quickstep and

disappearance. Over the earth's
wobble, eternity is a calculation.
Instead I write my name

in the dust along the windowsill,
the star's lost light falling across
the vase of flowers on the kitchen table.

for Donald Revell

Meditation on a Photograph of a Man Jumping a Huge Puddle in the Rain

The time: then. The spirit: always.
And the rain: now. Sometimes

the day will leave
something behind—what?—
something

between our toes
or under our last words at night.

We might say, "Let's go ahead,"
and we do. We leap. And the eyes
watching from

the corners and doorways
go on to what stays the same.

For now, we
are different. You
and I. And the rain

and time and the spinning world.

for Mark Hillringhouse

After Another Massacre

Night comes even
with evening.

Our cat lies
purring,
a supplication.

We will say
a prayer
for the cold rain,

for the trees
going skeletal.

Over in That Corner, the Puppets

Even when the weather changes,
remember to pet the dog, make
the cat purr, watch whatever

comes to the window. If you
stand there long enough,
someone will come by,

a stranger perhaps, one who
could be more, but needs
to keep walking. Hello—

likely all you can say.

for Naomi Shihab Nye

Another Day in Your Life

The thing is this rain keeps
falling and the long notion
of another day stays

relentless as a ringing phone.
What if you made up who you are
and why your mother never ate cereal,

why your father was a night watchman
in his own home? You keep things
tidy and full of happy endings. You

rearrange the empty jars in the cellar,
remembering the way you strained
the apricots, blueberries, raspberries,

how you stirred the apple butter, sealed
and labeled each jar. You sort through
the gladiolus bulbs lying on frayed window

screens, pull off new tubers, count them
to see if you'll have three or four times
as many in the summer when the wheat

grass around your house has grown
so thick the cats can hide. You swipe
the webs from corners of the windows,

go back upstairs, sit down with a drink,
the windows open, and you smile as you tell
yourself the same old jokes your father told.

Things Are Never the Same

Let's say you like birdhouses. Let's say
you like birds, too. Roaming through
the antique mall that took over
the Church of the Last Christ Jesus

that had taken over the Spinning Lights
Roller Rink where twenty years ago
you wished you didn't have a lisp and
didn't have to skate alone when

the baritone crooned, "Alllllllll
skate. All skate." Let's say you find
a two-story Victorian perfect for wrens,
sparrows, or goldfinches, a stern Shaker

round-walled barn just right for grackles,
two slant-roofed boxes made to welcome
wood ducks, seven gourds that will sway
from branches rocking chickadees,

juncos, and nuthatches, and a high-rise
apartment for a cult of purple martins.
What is one, two, seven more to hang
with the others hooked over the branches

of the maples, oaks, hemlocks, birches,
sycamores, and your one curly willow?

for Mary Ruefle

Within What You Endure

Beneath the quilt you lie
still in the chronic morning

light, eyes on the ceiling's blank
canvas. You paint your father

in a dark blue shirt kneeling
in his garden, you sitting small

beside him, he handing you
his trowel and a seedling,

as if to say, "You plant this one."
And you imagine you do. Then

you paint your own house
half built at the foot of a gentle

rise within the quiet landscape
of a stagger of pines higher

than the roof. The sun is halfway
up. You put down your brush

and welcome the day, your day
spreading out into its question.

After Hearing the Professor Say, "She's Just an Average Student"

How great never to be that bully
excellent. Not even the bland
and shy acolyte good. Average,
simply average, like all the robins,

jays, juncos, chickadees. Even
wood ducks, those charmingly
helmeted harlequins who never
arrive without floating a surprise

over any creek or pond, are average
when it comes to wood ducks.
Elephants, unless they rival the heft
and height of Jumbo are, well, average

elephants. The experts, of course, determine
what is above average, whether elephant
or student, while trillium, sweet woodruff,
owls, moles, goldenrod, and thyme hold

to the way they became. They cannot rise
to the rigor of demand or slough off into
a lower caste. Those who know say
wedding veil is indeed an excellent vine,

argue its worth over, say, euonymus.
But euonymus is always euonymus.
Wisteria is wisteria, just as English ivy
is English ivy, the former cascading

through a pergola, the latter climbing
and twisting its way up the side of a
wall, a tree. So come and let's redeem
the average. After all, for all I know,

I am an average coffee drinker here
on an average early morning watching
an average squirrel searching for all
the average acorns in our average yard,

readying for yet another average winter.

Some Answers to Your Question

—No.

—Only when the door is unlocked and open.

—Oh, I suppose it's simply the way I am.

—My mother.

—Well, the Bible seems to, at least to my mind, contradict itself on that.

—I think it was after he fell off his bicycle. The bike, by the way, was ruined.

—Do I really think so? Is that any question to ask? I mean really.

—Don't worry about it. They're like that.

Some Notes I Took
This Morning

Some say naming separates one
from another; then we see.

Light on the day lilies. That's a name
I like. I hadn't realized that before.

Snow. Snow. Snow.   Snow.

Our dog pulls and twists
and pushes and scrapes
at the blanket on the daybed,
then lies down.

Throwing things away is good. Not
throwing things away is also good.

Am I naming?

The dissonance of birds singing
braids the air. Kingfisher and song sparrow?

Sometimes I know why I wash the windows:
I hear voices.

There cannot be a better word for lunch than lunch.

It's Christmas

I heard someone say, "Again," and the anonymous
stars burned down the way our daughter made her
way down the alley behind our house. But the old

carols stayed, and the old songs sung off-key stayed
off the charts. Meanings matter only to the anodyne
of intellect. Believing is irrelevant, mere panache

beside the mystery. Oh, it's crucial to those who
need its winter coat, vital to those who insist there
is nothing. Both leave the days in their own wake.

Today we're going to every store in town. We'll buy
everything. We'll give it all away, wrapped in last
month's news. We'll stop by the manger, say hello,

and offer that we did our best. Back home we'll pile up
apples, pears, tangelos, and kumquats, hang a wreath
on the back door, lock the front door on anyone selling

chances or guarantees, on anyone asking us to ring a bell.
If it snows we'll tow our sleds to the top of McGuire's Hill,
take a running start, and just like last year make it all the way

down, then head back to the bourbon in the cabinet,
the trays of dates and frosted gingerbread sheep, cows,
and donkeys on the kitchen counter. We will pretend

to pray, knowing we can always stay off-key.

for D. R. James

Putting Down Our Dogs

We let the vet
place them

on the last place
they will smell.

Do they see
the unknown

in our eyes?
They feel

our fingers
scratch

behind
their ears.

Then our palms
along their backs.

At the Far End of Town Where the River Bends

A muskrat hulks
on the shore, looks
at me,

doesn't
move.

No matter where we are going,
we are
wandering. Even here at home—

Room to room. Into

the kitchen where
a drawer is filled
with a tangle of whisks, knives, and spatulas.

Into

the living room, the books
haphazard, wide along the wall.

Or carrying a purpose
into the garage, the garden.

Sometimes we are sitting,
not waiting. And something
comes or maybe
it's just that it has always
been there.

The muskrat sits. A willow's straggle
of yellow leaves draping
behind him.

Keeping the Windows Open

When the television's blue haze
sends you the distraction of America,

the holy sound of the wind chime
will find its way.

Window. Back porch. Candle. Desk drawer.

Perhaps you look up from the language
of your work to see the heron, in the joy
of no expectance, standing, still,
in the bend of the stream, and you feel
your past as seamless as water.

The great bird may then lift and carry
its feathered cross deep into the eye's horizon,
its body as still as when it stood, its wings
bringing their certainty of rhythm into the air.

Our own lives now stand along
that same stream.

Behind them,

the mute stars,

our whispers

                                       for a festschrift for Jacob Nyenhuis

Guided Meditation

Sit in a way that allows you to be comfortable
and relaxed. Do not let this hot and humid morning
enter your mind. Empty your mind, even if you

were up until 3 a.m. trying to forget what
your doctor told you yesterday afternoon. Now
take three deep breaths, allowing yourself

to savor the mysterious gift that you
are breathing. You are breathing here
during this one moment, the only moment

that the benevolence of the earth gives
during this moment. This is your moment
even though we do not yet know

what a moment is. I often wonder what
the moment is just prior to the moment.
But that is a thought. And this is a yoga

meditation, and we are to accept each thought
as simply something that passes through us
and goes on its merry, or often unmerry, way.

Take another breath, counting to four on the inhale
while picturing a gnome strolling up your nostrils
lugging a bag of gentle breezes, then count to six

on the exhale as the gnome cascades ass over
essential oils on an avalanche of air. Feel
your whole body fully relaxed. Continue breathing.

Picture a candle in a cave. Do not ask why in the
whole wide world there is a candle in a cave. If
you do, see in the question a yogi smiling as he

searches for the matches. Continue breathing.
And now imagine a field of lotus flowers. Or
if you are from the Midwest and unfamiliar

with lotus flowers you can always substitute corn.
Now picture rain on a roof. Listen to it. Listen
to the distant cough of thunder. Just listen. Do not

think about what you left out to ruin the last time
it rained. Continue breathing, and as you do, allow
any image to appear on the multiplex of your mind.

Be sure not to fixate on any one image. If a lover
old or new comes at you with a flamethrower, just
sit, watch, let it all pass, be glad your ego's been emulsified.

Stay relaxed. Continue breathing. Feel the comfort
of your whole body as you repeat the mantra, "I am
at peace. I am totally at peace. I am really, totally at peace."

Now that you are at peace, feel your feet, palms, pelvic floor
fully at rest in the room. Come to Sukhasana. Bring your hands
to your heart and join me for one long peaceful Ommmmmmmmm.

for Ami, Stacy, and Teresa

To This New Child Breathing in the World

The world's slow promise
waits for
your walk, the next

chance to wander along
each day's concert
of impossible notes. Your

mother, audacious with
love, is in your blood. She
will sleep in your bones. She

will look up into the sky's long
reach and ask that you stay longer
than the day her father had, safer

than her mother lives. And you
will carry their fierce and loyal
quiet. Yes, you will bring him

back, and with them walk
within the light between the trees.
You will step to the edge

of the garden and see
what Cézanne saw—no line:
the blending of form

with form and color, feel
the wild uncertain weight
of their hearts' unruly kindness.

for Anne Harrington Hughes and Jane Harrington Bach

If You're Waiting, You May
As Well . . .

One Wednesday, God joined
Calder's circus. She stepped into
the ring and asked the elephant
to lower its great and bewildered head.
God sat and the elephant rose
and walked.

Now we walk around, sometimes talking,
sometimes stopping to look or buy.
The sun takes away even its trace.

My grandfather loved to laugh.
He spent his last year dying, retelling
every gentle joke he knew. Downstairs,
my grandmother made her way between
each meal. My mother carried me
within her. My grandfather died at Christmas.
I was born in early April.

Sometimes when the air is light,
God lies back on the elephant, and
the hands of everyone turn to milk.
They rise, or reach, or decide to fold.

During World War II my father drove
his truck through Belgium and France.
He believed the war would never end.
My mother, as she nursed me,
listened for his voice.

God leans down, tries to listen.
The music is too loud.

Now my daughter has put away her toys. Now
she is learning to wait.

And now my father wakes early, goes out
to his garden and all day
works its soil, stopping only
for meals, a conversation, or
another delicious task.

Sometimes when the sky stays blue,
my mother looks out the kitchen window
and sees us all standing in the garden.

God's enormous loneliness covers us.

And the elephant's tongue tastes
the sweet, dry sacrifice of straw.

Morning Again

This poem will not be
anything new, will slowly
make its way across
the page and down, a walk
from here to somewhere
later on where it will
take its place quietly,
I hope, with the leaves,
the dog asleep on the porch,
the way the garden keeps giving
us plants, the way the wind
is invisible, the way none of us
can ever know for sure.

Let Comfort Come

We read while form stays
still and waits. The words sing
or speak, clamor on or say

or tell or even sometimes step
aside and hope we wander in.
Everywhere within the form

of letter, word, space, structure
rests the hush around the hurry,
the opening wherein any form—

table, door, the lover's arm
and tongue, the cat asleep
on the sill—lies the quiet,

the shawl around us all
who have to clatter through.
Let it be the nothing of not.

Why We Stay

I am on the porch with strong coffee.
All the artists, poets, philosophers with
no reasons, and the haphazard gardeners

are sleeping in or waking to their visions.
At the feeder—the first birds of the morning:
chickadees in their black-and-white cassocks,

the house finches, their muted red scarves
head to shoulder, nuthatches upside down.
This is the way the day is to be—loved

without definition. Joy known without
needing sorrow. It is only quiet, first
light moving in its unencumbered way

across each leaf, branched or fallen. Deep
in itself the earth trembles, our own way
lost and lingering at an unfelt edge.

Acknowledgments

With everlasting gratitude to the editors of the following publications in which many of these poems first appeared, some in a different form: *Artful Dodge, Burningword, Chariton Review, Colorado Review, Diner, 5AM, Free Lunch, Georgia Review, Gulf Coast, Harpur Palate, I-70 Review, Journal, Listening Eye, Louisville Review, Michigan Quarterly, Moria, Peninsula Poets, Poet Lore, Poetry, Poetry East, Poetry Society of Michigan, Rattapallax, Rattle, A Ritual to Read Together: Poems in Conversation with William Stafford, San Pedro River Review, Scintilla, Southern Poetry Review, Sport Literate, Talking River Review, Tar River Review, Temenos, 3288 Review, Third Coast, Third Wednesday, Waymark,* and *Yarrow.*

Special thanks to Paul Zimmer, who started it all. It's his fault.

Thank you to Jane Harrington Bach, Greg Rappleye, Conrad Hilberry, John and Jackie Bartley, Colette Volkema DeNooyer, D. L. James, D. R. James, Jim Allis, Jane and James Ashbrook Perkins, Nancy E. James, Sue and Nelson Oestreich, Michael Delp, Norbert Kraas, Todd Davis, Linda Nemec Foster, Chris Dombrowski, Christian Zaschke, The Family Garlinghouse, The Family Ridl, Naomi Shihab Nye (who taught me to say "yes"), and the soulful members of the Landscapes of Poetry. Thank you to Mark Hiskes, Rebecca Klot, and Rosemerry Wahtola Trommer, who know why.

I am grateful to my students at the college who gave me such rich days, to the editors of the magazines who affirmed the poems, and to all those I have overlooked.

Finally, much appreciation for the sustaining care of one and all at Wayne State University Press—Kristina Stonehill, Rachel Ross, Theresa Martinelli, Jamie Jones, Emily Nowak, and Carrie Teefey—and for the great, good, intelligent heart of my editor, Annie Martin.

About the Author

Jack Ridl's *Practicing to Walk Like a Heron* (Wayne State University Press, 2013) was awarded the Gold Medal for Poetry by *ForeWord Reviews*. His collection *Broken Symmetry* (Wayne State University Press, 2006) was co-recipient of the Society of Midland Authors Best Book of Poetry Award. Winner of the Gary Gildner Prize for Poetry, Jack also received the Talent Award from the Literacy Society of West Michigan for his "lifetime of work for poetry literacy," and the Poetry Society of Michigan named him "honorary chancellor," only the second poet so honored. Jack and his wife, Julie, founded the visiting writers series at Hope College, where he taught for thirty-seven years. More than ninety of his former students are now published authors.